INVENTORS WHO CHANGED THE WORLD

Angela Royston

Crabtree Publishing Company

www.crabtreebooks.com

Author: Angela Royston
Editor: Kathy Middleton
Production coordinator: Ken Wright
Prepress technician: Margaret Amy Salter
Series consultant: Gill Matthews

Picture Credits:
Alamy Images: Pictorial Press Ltd 24
Apple: 27b
Corbis: Hulton-Deutsch Collection: Cover br, Ted Soqui 26
Fotolia: Comugnero Silvana 23r
Getty Images: The Bridgeman Art Library/John Seymour Lucas 8
Istockphoto: Kkgas 23l, Marco Maccarini 19b,
     Chris Price 15t, Duncan Walker 9
Library of Congress: 14, 20l, 20r, 21, Detroit Publishing Company
     Photograph Collection 15b, Raff & Gammon 13
Photolibrary: North Wind Picture Archives 7
Rex Features: Roger-Viollet 6
Shutterstock: Cover, Aquatic Creature 5, Robert Hardholt 27t,
     Denis Klimov 25b, Emin Kuliyev 11b, Margot Petrowski 29
U.S. Air Force: 25t
Wikimedia Commons: 4, 10, 11t, 12t, 12b, 16, 22, Maryland
     Newspaper Project 19t, Smithsonian Institution Libraries 18,
     Zenodot Verlagsgesellschaft mbH 17l, 17r
Wikipedia: Enrique Dans 28, Cover tr

Library and Archives Canada Cataloguing in Publication

Royston, Angela
     Inventors who changed the world / Angela Royston.

(Crabtree connections)
Includes index.
ISBN 978-0-7787-9902-3 (bound).--ISBN 978-0-7787-9923-8 (pbk.)

     1. Inventors--Biography--Juvenile literature.
2. Inventions--History--Juvenile literature.
I. Title. II. Series: Crabtree connections

T39.R69 2011   j609.2'2   C2010-905299-4

Library of Congress Cataloging-in-Publication Data

Royston, Angela, 1945-
     Inventors who changed the world / Angela Royston.
          p. cm. -- (Crabtree connections)
     Includes index.
     ISBN 978-0-7787-9923-8 (pbk. : alk. paper) -- ISBN 978-0-7787-9902-
     (reinforced library binding : alk. paper)
     1. Inventors--Biography--Juvenile literature. 2. Inventions--History
Juvenile literature. I. Title.
     T39.R694 2010
     609.2'2--dc22
                                                              2010032438

Crabtree Publishing Company
www.crabtreebooks.com   1-800-387-7650

Printed in the U.S.A./112013/CG20130917

Published in Canada
Crabtree Publishing
616 Welland Ave.
St. Catharines, Ontario
L2M 5V6

Published in the United States
Crabtree Publishing
PMB 59051
350 Fifth Avenue, 59th Floor
New York, New York 10118

CONTENTS

A Spark of Genius.. 4

James Watt... 6

George Stephenson... 8

Michael Faraday.. 10

Thomas Alva Edison.. 12

Alexander Graham Bell.. 14

Karl Benz.. 16

Guglielmo Marconi.. 18

The Wright Brothers... 20

Leo Baekeland... 22

Alan Turing.. 24

Martin Cooper.. 26

Tim Berners-Lee.. 28

Glossary.. 30

Further Information... 31

Index.. 32

A SPARK OF GENIUS

An invention is a machine or **device** that changes the way something is done. Most inventions change things a little bit at a time, but sometimes, a single invention can change people's lives.

> "Genius is one percent inspiration and ninety-nine percent **perspiration**."
>
> Thomas Edison

Changing the world

For thousands of years, people lived in villages, traveled on foot or by horse, and made things in small workshops. Today, most people live in cities and travel by car, train, and airplane. They have computers and many other electrical gadgets made in large factories. These huge changes are the result of just a few inventions.

▼ Until the 1800s, most people rode horses or walked from place to place. Only a few people traveled in horse-drawn carriages.

▲ *Today, wide streets are crowded with cars and buses.*

Solving problems

Inventors may not set out to change the world. James Watt (see page 6) was simply trying to make an existing steam engine work better. Guglielmo Marconi (see page 18) used the work of other scientists to invent a way of sending and receiving radio signals. He had no idea that his invention would lead to television and cell phones!

WHAT DOES IT TAKE?
Inventors often have the ability to see things in a different way than most people. This allows them to come up with totally new solutions. This is a true spark of genius.

JAMES WATT

< < T I M E L I N E > >

- **1736** Born on January 19 in Greenock, Scotland
- **1765** Invented a successful steam engine
- **1819** Died on August 25

"I can think of nothing but this engine."
James Watt

Watt's steam engine was used in factories, trains, and ships. It changed the way people worked and traveled.

▼ James Watt

James Watt enjoyed mathematics at school, and his father taught him **carpentry**. He trained in making mathematical instruments and found work at Glasgow University.

Inventing a new engine

In 1763 the university asked him why the steam engines that were used in coal mines needed so much steam. The answer came to Watt quite suddenly, when he was out walking one Sunday in May 1765. He designed a new engine in his head and made a small **model** of it the next day. It used much less steam than the existing engine.

Success

Watt then made a full-size engine, but it kept leaking steam. It took him nine years to solve these problems. By then, he had formed a company with Matthew Boulton. In 1776, the first Boulton–Watt engine was installed in a coal mine. It worked perfectly! Boulton then encouraged Watt to **adapt** his engine so that it could be used by machines in factories.

RICH AND FAMOUS

By 1800, 84 cotton mills in England were using Watt's new engine to turn cotton into fabric. Watt became famous and wealthy.

▼ *Factories using Watt's steam engines were built across Britain.*

GEORGE STEPHENSON

<< T I M E L I N E >>

- **1781** Born on June 9 in Wylam, near Newcastle-upon-Tyne, England
- **1829** Invented *Rocket*, the first passenger railway **locomotive**
- **1848** Died on August 12

▼ *George Stephenson*

The success of Stephenson's *Rocket* led to railway tracks being laid across Britain, and later across the world.

Even as a child, George Stephenson was interested in machines. When he grew up, he worked in several coal mines. In his spare time, he took apart the mine engines to see how they worked. Then he began to build his own machines. In 1814 he built a steam locomotive that could haul 30 tons (27 metric tons) of coal along metal rail tracks.

Locomotion

George formed a company with his son Robert and built a faster locomotive called *Locomotion*. In 1825 *Locomotion* was used to haul coal on a new railway line between Stockton and the port of Darlington.

"By the time the [train] arrived at Stockton, where it was received with great joy, there were not less than 600 persons within, and hanging by the carriages."

John Sykes, who watched the opening of the Stockton and Darlington Railway

ROCKETING TO SUCCESS

In 1829 a competition called the Rainhill Trials was held to choose a locomotive to pull passenger trains between Liverpool and Manchester. Stephenson entered *Rocket*, a new locomotive, and it won the competition!

3. The Rocket.

▲ *A sketch of an early steam train inspired by Stephenson's* Rocket

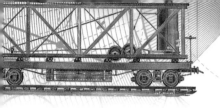

MICHAEL FARADAY

< < TIMELINE > >

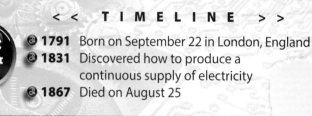

- **1791** Born on September 22 in London, England
- **1831** Discovered how to produce a continuous supply of electricity
- **1867** Died on August 25

"Nothing is too wonderful to be true, if it be consistent with the laws of nature."

Michael Faraday

Faraday invented an electric **generator** and an **electric motor**. All the electrical equipment we plug in and use today is based on his work.

Michael Faraday's father was a **blacksmith**, and Faraday was poorly educated. When he was 14, he became an **apprentice** to a **bookbinder**. Faraday loved reading, and he educated himself by reading the books he bound, particularly the science books.

◀ *Michael Faraday*

Help from Humphry

In 1812 Faraday began to attend lectures given by the famous scientist Humphry Davy. When Davy's eyesight was damaged in an accident, he employed Faraday as his secretary and scientific assistant. In 1813 Davy recommended Faraday for a job at the **Royal Institution**.

▲ *Humphry Davy*

▼ *Today we use electricity for lighting and to run many machines.*

MOTORS AND GENERATORS

While Faraday was helping Davy, he began his own investigations. He showed that it is possible to **generate** electricity by moving a magnet inside a coil of wire. This discovery allowed Faraday to invent an electric motor and a generator, which together made electricity into a powerful source of energy.

THOMAS ALVA EDISON

< < TIMELINE > >

1847 Born on February 11 in Milan, Ohio
1876 Set up an inventions laboratory in Menlo Park, New Jersey, where he invented the lightbulb
1931 Died October 18

▼ *An exhausted Edison and his phonograph in 1888*

Edison's inventions included many things that we now take for granted, such as electric lighting.

Thomas Edison was a curious and lively child. He was too lively to fit in at school, so his mother taught him at home. He was always eager to try new experiments to see what would happen.

◀ *Thomas Alva Edison as a boy*

Inventive mind

When he grew up, Edison had so many ideas for inventions that he set up an inventions factory at Menlo Park in New Jersey, where he then lived. The most famous invention that he developed at Menlo Park was the electric light. He not only invented a successful lightbulb, he designed everything else that was needed, from light switches to electricity **meters**.

EDISON THE SHOWMAN

To **publicize** his invention of electric light, he invited important people to a grand opening. Edison laid electric cables to one area in New York. Everyone waited in the dark until the whole area slowly lit up when the electricity began to flow. Edison's fame spread around the world.

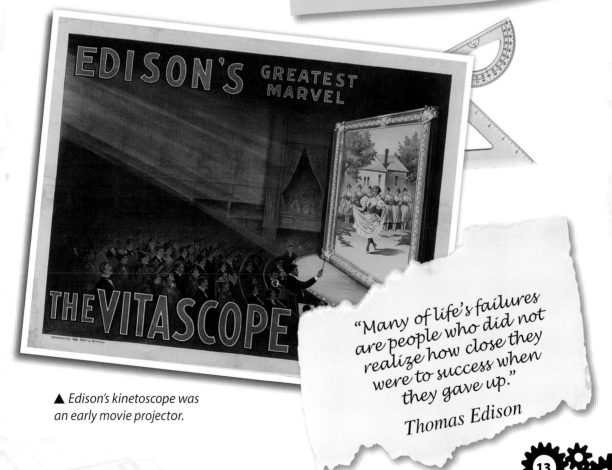

▲ Edison's kinetoscope was an early movie projector.

"Many of life's failures are people who did not realize how close they were to success when they gave up."

Thomas Edison

ALEXANDER GRAHAM BELL

<< TIMELINE >>

- **1847** Born on March 3 in Edinburgh, Scotland
- **1876** Invented the telephone
- **1922** Died on August 2

Telephones allowed people to communicate instantly, even when separated by long distances.

"Writing ... is a slow and tedious way of expressing myself. I long for one of our old confabulations [chats]."

From a letter written by Alexander Graham Bell to a friend

Bell was always interested in the way the human voice made sounds. As a teenager, he even managed to get the family dog to growl in a way that sounded like speech!

◄ *Alexander Graham Bell*

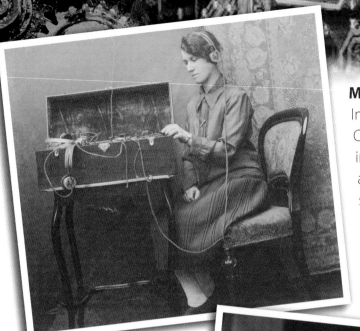

Moving to Canada

In 1870 the family moved to Canada. Bell was interested in the **telegraph**, which was a way of sending electrical signals along a wire using **Morse code**. Bell, however, wanted to send and receive speech, so that he could actually talk to his friends.

▲ *An operator sends and receives messages using Morse code.*

Inventing the telephone

The telegraph made signals by turning a current on and off. In 1874 Bell got the idea of changing the strength of the electrical current to be like speech. With the help of Thomas Watson, an **electrical engineer**, he developed his idea. He made a great number of experiments and finally, in March 1876, he succeeded.

▲ *This early telephone has a trumpet for listening to the incoming call.*

PHONES FOR EVERYONE
Bell set up the Bell Telephone Company and began to supply phones to the public.

KARL BENZ

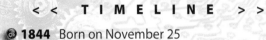

< < T I M E L I N E > >

- **1844** Born on November 25 in Karlsruhe, Germany
- **1885** Invented the first successful automobile fueled by gasoline
- **1929** Died on April 4

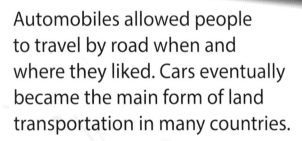

Automobiles allowed people to travel by road when and where they liked. Cars eventually became the main form of land transportation in many countries.

When he was young, Karl Benz dreamed of producing a "horseless carriage"—a vehicle that would power itself. He studied **mechanical engineering** at university.

◀ *Karl Benz*

▼ *Several inventors came up with sketches for early cars. This is one of them.*

▲ *The first cars were open to the wind and cold, and they frequently broke down.*

Benz's three-wheeler

In 1883 Benz set up Benz & Company in Mannheim. There he began to develop engines that were powered by burning gasoline. He also invented all the mechanical parts that he needed to build his first automobile, including the gears and a way of starting the engine. He drove his three-wheeled automobile through Mannheim in 1885, and in 1886 he obtained a **patent** for it.

BERTHA'S FAMOUS DRIVE

Benz's wife Bertha helped to make the car famous. In 1888, she drove it for 66 miles (106 km). There were no gas stations at that time, but gas was sold as a cleaning product in **pharmacies**. Bertha had to keep stopping to buy more gas! But she proved that the car could be driven for long distances.

GUGLIELMO MARCONI

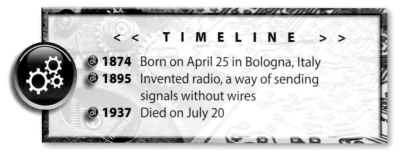

<< **T I M E L I N E** >>

- **1874** Born on April 25 in Bologna, Italy
- **1895** Invented radio, a way of sending signals without wires
- **1937** Died on July 20

As a child, Guglielmo was always interested in science. When he failed to get into university, he decided to study at home. He was fascinated by Heinrich Hertz's discovery that invisible waves could be **transmitted** without wires across a room.

Today radio signals are used to **broadcast** radio and television programs and to send cellphone messages around the world.

▼ *Guglielmo Marconi*

Increasing distance

Marconi experimented with these invisible waves until he was able to transmit and receive signals over one mile (1.6 km). Since the Italian government was not interested in his invention, he traveled to London in 1896. Here he got backing and a patent for his wireless telegraph.

Over the next few years he sent and received signals over longer and longer distances. In 1901 he managed to send a signal from England to Newfoundland— all the way across the Atlantic Ocean!

▲ *Many passengers were saved when the Titanic sank in 1912, because the ship broadcast radio distress signals.*

SPREAD OF RADIO

At first Marconi's wireless telegraph was used mainly by ships. Later other scientists discovered how to use radio signals to transmit the human voice, and in the 1920s, the first radio stations began broadcasting music for entertainment.

▶ *The first radio signal to cross the Atlantic was received here at St. John's Hill, in Newfoundland.*

THE WRIGHT BROTHERS

< < TIMELINE > >

- **1867** Wilbur Wright born on April 16 in Milville, Indiana
- **1871** Orville Wright born on August 19 in Dayton, Ohio
- **1903** Invented an airplane powered by an engine
- **1912** Wilbur died on May 30
- **1948** Orville died on January 30

"If birds can glide for long periods of time, then ... why can't I?"

Orville Wright

The Wright brothers made the first successful airplane flight. Their work has made it possible for people to fly all over the world.

▼ *Orville Wright*

▲ *Wilbur Wright*

▲ *Orville Wright's first flight, made near Kitty Hawk in North Carolina, lasted just 12 seconds.*

Even as children the Wright brothers were good at making machines. When they left school, they opened a bicycle shop and sold bicycles they had made themselves.

Experiments with flying

A few people had already flown **gliders**. The Wright brothers experimented to find a way of steering the glider by moving the wings. Then they designed and built an engine.

THE FIRST FLIGHT

By 1903 the Wrights had attempted to fly several times and failed. Then on December 17 they tried again. This time the plane lifted off the ground and flew 120 feet (37 m). The age of powered flight had arrived!

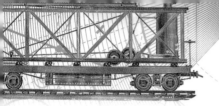

LEO BAEKELAND

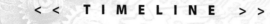

- **1863** Born on November 14 near Ghent, Belgium
- **1907** Developed Bakelite, the first completely **synthetic** plastic
- **1944** Died on February 23

"It was kind of an accident, because plastic is not what I meant to invent."

Leo Baekeland

Leo Baekeland's synthetic material led to all the many kinds of plastic we use today.

Leo Baekeland studied **chemistry** at the University of Ghent, but when he was 26 he moved to New York in the United States. Here he invented a new kind of photographic paper, which he called Velox.

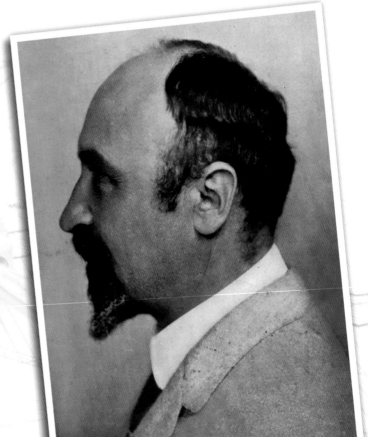

▶ *Leo Baekeland*

Almost a millionaire

In 1898 he sold his invention of Velox to a photographic company for $750,000. The money meant that he never had to work again! Instead he spent his time experimenting with new synthetic materials.

Old Faithful

He heated different substances in a kind of pressure cooker, which he called "Old Faithful." While he was trying to find a better way to produce **asbestos**, he discovered a new substance, which he called Bakelite.

BAKELITE

Bakelite could be easily molded into any shape, so it was made into many different things, from knife handles to telephones. It was particularly useful in making cars and electrical products. Baekeland became a multimillionaire!

▼ *An early gramophone plays a record made of Bakelite.*

▲ *A telephone made of Bakelite*

ALAN TURING

< < T I M E L I N E > >

1912	Born on June 23 in London, England
1945–54	Developed much of the basic technology used in computers
1954	Died on June 7

▼ Alan Turing

Alan Turing's work paved the way for the development of the computer, an invention that revolutionized the way people work, communicate, and play.

Alan Turing was a mathematical genius. After Turing graduated from Cambridge University he went on to study codes and code-breaking at Princeton University in the United States. He returned to Britain in 1938, just before World War II began.

Secret service

During the war, Turing worked as a code-breaker for the British secret service. He built a machine called "Bombe." It helped break the complex code called Enigma used by the Germans to communicate with their submarines.

First computers

After the war, Turing worked on the design for an Automatic Computing Engine (ACE). His design would have worked, but his **colleagues** were not convinced. ACE was never built. However, Turing developed much of the science that makes today's computers possible.

▶ *This is a replica of Alan Turing's original Bombe, which could test millions of possible codes very quickly.*

"A computer would deserve to be called intelligent if it could deceive a human into believing that it was human."

Alan Turing

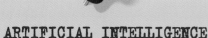

ARTIFICIAL INTELLIGENCE

Turing was also interested in artificial intelligence— a computer that can think, rather than just carry out instructions. This has still not been achieved.

◀ *Asimo is a modern robot that can do some of the things humans can do.*

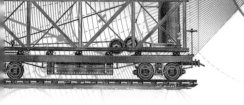

MARTIN COOPER

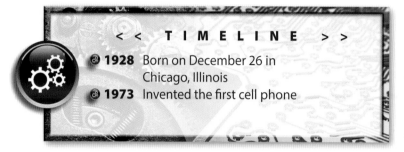

< < T I M E L I N E > >

- **1928** Born on December 26 in Chicago, Illinois
- **1973** Invented the first cell phone

Martin Cooper studied electrical engineering at university before joining the U.S. Navy during the Korean War. After the war, he worked at Teletype and then moved to Motorola in 1954.

Cell phones are changing people's lives around the world. Today cell phones can access the **Internet**, and take and transmit photographs and videos.

"People want to talk to other people—not a house, or an office, or a car."

Martin Cooper

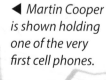

◀ *Martin Cooper is shown holding one of the very first cell phones.*

From car phones to cell phones

In the 1970s, Cooper was put in charge of designing car phones. He wanted to develop a phone that was small enough to be carried around outside the car as well as inside. It took Cooper and his engineers just three months to produce the first model in 1973.

▲ *Cell phones can be used in places where there are no telephone wires.*

FIRST CALL

On April 3, 1973, Cooper used his handheld phone in the street. People were amazed to see him walking down the street speaking on a telephone. Over the next 10 years cell phones became smaller and lighter. In 1983 the first cell phones were sold to the public.

▲ *Today's cell phones are mini computers.*

TIM BERNERS-LEE

< < **TIMELINE** > >

- **1955** Born on June 8 in London, England
- **1989–91** Invented the World Wide Web

"Sites need to be able to interact in one single, universal space."

Tim Berners-Lee

The World Wide Web is a part of the Internet that holds a vast library of information available to everyone.

As a child, Tim Berners-Lee was fascinated by encyclopedias, computers, and how people acquired knowledge. While he was at Oxford University studying physics, he made his own computer, using a television set, a **microprocessor**, and a **soldering iron**.

▶ Tim Berners-Lee

Sharing information

In the 1980s Berners-Lee was working at **CERN** in Switzerland, when he came up with the idea of linking files so that people around the world could easily share reports and other information. He called the system "Enquire." Then in 1989 he developed a way of linking documents that made it easy for users to find information instantly. The World Wide Web was born and became available on the Internet in 1991.

NOT RICH OR FAMOUS

Tim Berners-Lee could have made a fortune from his invention, but he chose not to. He was more concerned that the information on the Web remain free and available to everyone.

▲ *The World Wide Web can be* **accessed** *from anywhere in the world.*

GLOSSARY

access Ability to get or use something

adapt Change something to fit something else

apprentice Someone who is learning a skill or craft by working alongside a skilled person

asbestos Substance that does not burn

blacksmith Person who makes horseshoes, tools, and other things made of iron

bookbinder Person who binds together the pages and covers of books

broadcast To send a program or some information using radio or television

carpentry Skill of building with wood and repairing things made of wood

CERN European Organization for Nuclear Research's center for scientific research

chemistry Study of the simple substances that combine together to make up all the substances in the world

colleagues People who work in the same field

device Something invented for a purpose

electrical engineer Person who works with electrical machines

electric motor Engine that is powered by electricity

generate Create or bring into being

generator Machine that produces electricity

gliders Lightweight aircraft with small motors

Internet Network that links computers around the world

locomotive Engine that pulls wagons and carriages along a railway track

mechanical engineering Branch of engineering that deals with machines

meters Instruments for measuring something, such as the amount of electricity used

microprocessor Tiny piece of silicon that contains many of the programs and processes required by a computer

model Small-scale version of something

Morse code Code that uses long and short sounds, or dots and dashes, to represent the letters of the alphabet

patent Legal document that gives an inventor the right to stop other people from using his or her invention without paying for it

perspiration Sweat

pharmacies Places where medicines are prepared and sold

publicize To make public or tell people about something

Royal Institution Organization based in London that encourages research in science

soldering iron Tool that uses hot metal to join two pieces of metal

synthetic Made from chemicals

telegraph Communication by sending electrical signals along an electric wire

transmitted Sent through space

FURTHER INFORMATION

Web Sites

Read biographies of some of the most famous inventors at:
library.thinkquest.org/5847/halloffame.htm

Search for information about different inventors in the National Inventors Hall of Fame at:
www.invent.org/hall_of_fame/1_1_search.asp

Read a biography of Alexander Graham Bell with links to other websites about him at:
www.alexandergrahambell.org

There is a detailed biography of George Stephenson at:
www.spartacus.schoolnet.co.uk/RAstephensonG.htm

A biography of Guglielmo Marconi can be found at:
nobelprize.org/nobel_prizes/physics/laureates/1909/marconi-bio.html

Read an account of the Wright brothers and their historic first flight at:
www.biographyshelf.com/wright_brothers_biography.html

Books

Breakthrough Inventions Series. Crabtree Publishing Company (2007).

Inventions and Inventors by Darren Sechrist. Crabtree Publishing Company (2009).

Inventors' Secret Scrapbook by Chris Oxlade. Crabtree Publishing Company (2011).

INDEX

airplanes 4, 20–21
artificial intelligence 25
Automatic Computing Engine (ACE) 25

Baekeland, Leo 22–23
Bakelite 23
Bell, Alexander Graham 14–15
Benz, Karl 16–17
Berners-Lee, Tim 28–29

car phones 27
cars 4, 5, 16–17, 27
cell phones 5, 26–27
CERN 29
coal mines 6, 7, 8
code-breaking 24, 25
computers 24–25, 27, 28, 29
Cooper, Martin 26–27

Edison, Thomas Alva 12–13
electric cables 13
electric motor 10, 11
electricity 10, 11, 12, 13, 15
electricity meters 13
engines 6–7, 8–9, 17

factories 4, 6, 7, 13
Faraday, Michael 10–11

generator 10, 11
gliders 21

hypertext 29

kinetoscope 13

Internet 29

lightbulb 13
Locomotion 9
locomotives 8–9

Marconi, Guglielmo 5, 18–19
materials 22–23
Morse code 15

patent 17, 19
phonograph 12

radio 18–19
railway line 9
Rocket 8, 9

steam engines 5, 6–7
Stephenson, George 8–9

telegraph 15
telephones 5, 14–15, 23, 26–27
trains 4, 6, 8–9
travel 4–5, 16–17
Turing, Alan 24–25

Velox 22–23

Watt, James 5, 6–7
waves 18–19
World Wide Web 28–29
Wright brothers 20–21